Old ARBROATH

by
Fiona Scharlau

Cobb's Cycle Depot was located in this shed adjacent to the old tollhouse (also visible in the picture on page 35). From the late nineteenth century until World War I the fashion was for holidays in the fresh air, with walking tours or trips to the seaside particularly popular. The advent of the safety cycle in the 1890s greatly increased the popularity of cycling as a pastime. While richer tourists might bring their own cycles by train, many poorer folk would rent a bicycle for the day when they reached their destination. This picture suggests that Cobb's rented out motorcycles as well as push-bikes.

First published in the United Kingdom, 2001,
reprinted 2003, 2006, 2010
by Stenlake Publishing Limited,
01290 551122
www.stenlake.co.uk

ISBN 9781840330977

FURTHER READING

The publications listed below were used by the author during her research. None of them are available from Stenlake Publishing. Those interested in finding out more are advised to contact their local bookshop or reference library.

Arbroath Herald
Old Statistical Account of Scotland
New Statistical Account of Scotland
George Hay, *History of Arbroath to the Present Time*, Arbroath, 1876
George S. Shepherd, *Wir bookie o' the toon o' Arbroath*, Arbroath, 1993
George S. Shepherd, *Wir ither bookie o' the toon o' Arbroath*, Arbroath, 1993
Arbroath Abbey, Historic Scotland Guide
P. Charles Carragher, *Arbroath: Royal Burgh of Romance, its People and its Past*
J. M. McBain, *Arbroath Past and Present*, Arbroath, 1887
Margaret King, *An Auchmithie Album*, Forfar, 1991
Angus Archives research files

ACKNOWLEDGEMENTS

The author extends grateful thanks to the staff of Cultural Services and the Signal Tower Museum, Arbroath for answering her many questions. The help of Margaret King and Fiona Guest, former and present curators of the Signal Tower Museum, was especially appreciated.

The publishers would like to thank Alastair White for permission to use the pictures on page 37, and Robert Grieves for supplying the pictures on page 48 and the inside back cover.

Left: Asides from the attractions of the outdoor swimming pool (see page 26), beauty pageants were a favourite activity during the holiday season, and were held regularly from May to the end of September. The winner of the title 'Miss Arbroath' would receive the traditional tiara and sash plus a small gift. A junior Miss Arbroath competition was also held. This photograph shows Miss Arbroath September 1955 receiving her prizes from Mrs Napier.

Opposite: A Fifie leaving the harbour with the Signal Tower in the background. Fifies were sma' line boats used for catching haddock for smokie production. They were usually operated by families working together. Their sails were a rich brown colour derived from being immersed in a solution of bark extract to help prevent them from rotting.

INTRODUCTION

The town of Arbroath nestles on the east coast of Scotland midway between Dundee and Montrose. It was originally known as Aberbrothock because of its location on the Brothock Burn, but by the mid-nineteenth century the more colloquial spelling of Arbroath was being used.

Arbroath owes its existence to its abbey, established by King William the Lion in 1178 and dedicated to the memory of St Thomas a Becket. St Thomas was the patron saint of the town, and today the tomb of King William the Lion can be seen in the abbey. Arbroath Abbey consisted of 40 monks of the Tironesian order whose purpose was to perform divine service. A burgh of regality was established along with the abbey, giving the monks the right to hold a weekly market and to create a harbour, which they did in 1394. A village grew up surrounding the abbey to supply its needs and a fishing hamlet developed around the harbour.

Arbroath Abbey is internationally famous as the site of one of the key events in Scottish history. On 6 April 1320 Scotland's nobles gathered in the abbey to sign a declaration of Scottish independence addressed to the Pope. The abbey came to worldwide prominence again in 1951 when the Stone of Destiny, which had previously been stolen from Westminster Abbey, was discovered in front of its high altar, draped in a Saltire.

After the Reformation of the Roman Catholic Church in the 1560s, Arbroath Abbey was allowed to fall into decay, with its monks ignored and its buildings quarried for stone. In 1599 the town's rights and privileges were reconfirmed by King James VI in a charter of Novodamus, at which point it became a royal burgh. A provost, bailies, treasurer and a council were empowered to run its affairs. Trades Incorporations and a Merchants' Guildry were set up to regulate commerce and craftsmen.

For most of the following centuries, the small town of Arbroath had three principal streets, High Street, Marketgate, and Millgate. In 1742 its population numbered approximately 2,500. Fishing was important, as was the coastal shipping trade, while smuggling played a significant role in the vitality of the local economy during the eighteenth century. It was during the following century that Arbroath's economy received a boost from the Industrial Revolution. It had previously been developing as a centre for handloom weaving, and this industry was augmented by steam-powered flax, textile and engineering works which were built along the Brothock Burn. Sailcloth weaving alone supported 5,000 jobs and attracted many workers from the surrounding rural parishes. By 1875 there were 34 spinning mills and factories operating 1,400 power looms and producing 450,000 yards of cloth annually. In addition, bleachfields, tanneries, calendering works, asphalt and tar manufactories, chemical works and shipbuilding yards flourished. The large influx of workers resulted in Arbroath's growth, with the area once known as the Wyndies built especially to house handloom weavers. In 1839 the arrival of the railway allowed an easier two-way traffic in workers.

A new harbour of 1725 resulted in an increase in maritime trade. It was deeper than the previous anchorage and allowed larger ships to use the port, giving a boost to international trade. Arbroath's merchants responded enthusiastically. Fishing was vital to Arbroath for centuries, and from 1799 fishermen from the neighbouring village of Auchmithie were encouraged to relocate to the town's safer harbour by Arbroath Town Council. By 1826 only three fishing boats had taken up the offer, prompting the council to extend their offer to the fishing communities of Shetland and Inverbervie. Land for building homes was offered to the fishermen, who chose to settle at the foot of the town near the harbour. During the nineteenth century there was a steady drift from Auchmithie to Arbroath and by 1880 Arbroath's fishermen numbered 150. The fishing industry entered a serious decline in the twentieth century due to dwindling fish stocks, although the Arbroath smokie is still a much sought-after local product.

Today Arbroath is enjoying a resurgence of interest in its rich and varied heritage, as shown by the revival of the Arbroath Abbey Pageant and the establishment of Seafest. Robert Stevenson's Signal Tower is now a popular museum examining the many facets of Arbroath's rich ecclesiastical, industrial, and seafaring heritage.

A view over the lost streets of Ladyloan taken from the Signal Tower in 1965. In the distance on the hill is the water tower, constructed in 1885 by the unemployed in an early 'work for welfare' scheme. From a distance it looks like a Scottish baronial style castle. The tower contained three tanks that could hold 200,000 gallons of water for domestic use. Previously the people of Arbroath had been dependent for their water on a series of wells that served only a few streets. The water tower was only operational for 21 years.

The Ladyloan area of Arbroath was greatly altered by the building of the inner relief road in the 1960s, which necessitated the demolition of many streets. This 1921 aerial view shows the old main road through the town skirting round Ladyloan School. Gayfield, the home of the Red Lichties (as Arbroath's football team is affectionately known) was little more than a grass field at this stage. The large, two-storey, square building above the left goalpost (now demolished) is Gayfield House. On the hill at the far left-hand side is Windmill House, named after the windmill that once stood there. The house subsequently became a hotel and is now a Christian centre.

The part of Arbroath near the abbey was known as the Wyndies after streets such as Lillies Wynd and Cross Mill Wynd. It was made up of weavers' houses which had been built in the late eighteenth century to accommodate the influx of handloom weavers. Some of the houses were made of red sandstone reclaimed from the ruins of Arbroath Abbey. By the twentieth century they had fallen into a state of disrepair and were eventually pulled down during the 1950s and 1960s as part of a larger scheme of redevelopment. Council housing and part of the inner relief road now stand on their site. This picture shows the view up Smithy Croft from Cross Mill Wynd.

Another view of the Wyndies, showing the dormer windows of the upper stories where the male weavers worked. Their wives spun the yarn which they then worked into linen webs. Weavers were considered to be intelligent people and many managed to read while working the loom. From 1849 onwards handloom weaving began to be superseded by factory power looms.

The area at the bottom of the High Street is affectionately called the Fit o' the Toon. The large mansion in the foreground with the outside stair was once Lord Ogilvie's lodgings. Like many town houses that had once belonged to members of the gentry, it was eventually split up into a warren of one- or two-roomed houses, inhabited latterly by fisherfolk. Arbroath's fishing community originated in Auchmithie, but its members moved to Arbroath during the nineteenth century in pursuit of better living conditions and to use the safer harbour there.

These fine houses along the Shore directly overlook the harbour. They have changed little to this day, although the area in front of them has now been converted to a car park for visitors. Ship's captains, merchants and the harbour master once lived here, and the Smugglers Inn was formerly the customs house. Prior to 1830 when the town acquired its own customs facilities, all Arbroath vessels had to clear customs in Montrose before proceeding to Arbroath. Throughout the eighteenth century and during the early years of the nineteenth century, the smuggling of tobacco, brandy and other goods was rife along the length of the Angus coast. People from every level of society were involved in this trade, or condoned it by purchasing smuggled goods. Smuggling declined rapidly after the high duties imposed during the Napoleonic wars were lifted.

Freshly-landed catches of fish attract crowds to the harbourside. Much of the fish landed at Arbroath was caught using the sma' line method. The name is misleading, as the lines themselves were long and the term 'sma' referred to their thickness, not their length. Sma' line fishing took place all year round and was used to catch haddock and small white fish such as flukes and whiting. The lines were made of hemp and tipped with hooks baited with mussels or lugworms. Baiting the lines was women's work. Each member of a vessel's five-man crew supplied the boat with a scull of baited lines, each of which was about two miles in length.

The catch was always greeted by a host of eager purchasers on the quayside, the majority of whom were women. As a rule the fleet returned to harbour between midday and early evening – depending on the tide – having been at sea since before dawn. On their arrival crews needed time to clean their lines and replace missing hooks before going out to sea again the following day. With the exception of the skipper, who got an extra share for the upkeep of the boat, the day's catch was divided equally between each member of the crew.

The world-famous Arbroath smokie originated with the Auchmithie fishing community. The preparation of smokies involved hanging salted haddock in pairs over a barrel containing a fire of hardwood chips, which was dampened down by covering it with wet hessian. The smokies would be ready after about 45 minutes. In the summer of 2000 an ice cream seller in Arbroath introduced the smokie flavoured ice cream!

A fisher-girl plays with an umbrella on the beach. She is wearing clothes cut down from her mother's worn out ones and seems quite comfortable without shoes.

Arbroath lassies followed the fishing fleet when it travelled to Great Yarmouth and Scarborough for the July to September herring season; here they are seen 'heading up the barrels'. Catches of herring had to be salted within 24 hours to obtain the coveted Scottish Crown brand mark. Layers of fish and salt were added to the barrel before it was finally sealed with a wooden lid and the brand mark applied. It could take several days to fill a barrel in this way. Much of the catch was exported to the Baltic and Germany, but demand declined with the outbreak of World War I. The last herring catch landed in any quantity at Arbroath was in 1953.

Arbroath fisherwomen gathered at the bridge at the Fit o' the Toon beside Danger Point to do the weekly washing. They didn't need to undertake the laborious routine of wash day whereby a copper boiler was filled with water and brought to the boil; instead they took advantage of the plentiful supply of hot water that was discharged into the burn by the 30 or so flax mills and factories upstream on the Brothock Burn. In addition to washing their clothes, fishing paraphernalia such as sculls and mussel trouchs were scrubbed and cleaned.

THE HARBOUR, ARBROATH

A forest of masts filled Arbroath's harbour when the Fifie fishing boats berthed for the night. Arbroath has had a harbour since 1394 when the Abbot of Arbroath constructed one under royal charter. This was destroyed by a storm in 1706, and a new harbour was constructed from the beach and grassland at Ladyloan in 1795 at a cost of £6,000. It was successful in attracting trade to the town. Grain, salt, fish and paving stones were exported from the harbour while timber, iron and flax were imported. Trade began to decline in the mid-nineteenth century with the introduction of the faster and cheaper railway and the advent of steam ships. Many steam vessels were too large for Arbroath harbour, berthing in Dundee instead. The emphasis was switched from trade to fishing, an industry that has declined throughout the twentieth century.

The Signal Tower was built in 1813 and was once surrounded by a warren of houses and other buildings for the use of the masons and labourers working on the construction of the Bell Rock lighthouse. One of these houses was used by Robert Stevenson himself. The tower provided a home for the families of the lighthouse keepers, and messages could be communicated with the Bell Rock lighthouse by means of the signalling telescope – a brass ball which could be

THE SIGNAL TOWER, ARBROATH

moved up or down the pole it was attached to. An identical device was fitted to the lighthouse. Signals sent from the tower were sometimes of a very personal nature. When a baby was born to a lighthouse keeper on duty he was informed of the safe arrival and gender of his new child by the expedient of running a dress up the pole if it was a girl and a pair of trousers if it was a boy.

The Bell Rock has been a hazard to shipping for centuries, and according to legend the Abbot of Arbroath Abbey had a bell placed upon it to act as a warning of the danger it posed. Situated 11 miles out to sea, the rock barely dries out at low tide and is usually covered by between 4 and 12 feet of water. In the year that Robert Stevenson was appointed to the Northern Lighthouse Board, 70 ships were lost off the Bell Rock. Stevenson's Bell Rock lighthouse was one of the greatest civil engineering projects ever undertaken. Until the stone courses had been built above high water mark, work could only be conducted on the small amount of exposed rock for a few hours each day, and only then if the weather was good. Stevenson devised a unique three-dimensional interlocking plan for the new tower. Each stone was individually made for a particular place and pieced together on site like a jigsaw puzzle. The lighthouse became operational in February 1811.

The Bell Rock lighthouse underwent alterations in 1902 when the entire lantern and light was removed. A new paraffin light was installed with a fixed incandescent lamp, around which revolved the finest prismatic lenses then available. The ruby stained glass of the lamp continued to allow red and white flashes to be emitted. These pictures were taken during the 1902 alterations.

Queen and Princess Mary came to Arbroath on 8 September 1921 as part of a wider tour of Angus. They visited Arbroath Abbey and were given a guided tour by Provost Anderson and Abbey Keeper Enoch Bell. Afterwards they had lunch at Annesley House with Mrs Lindsay Carnegie, where Queen Mary planted a rosemary bush with the help of the gardener's daughter. The party continued to Kelly Castle for a guided tour before going on to Brechin Castle. The photograph shows the Queen's party leaving the abbey after their visit.

In 1934 Alexander Napier, proprietor of Scott's Grocers on the High Street (see page 40) and standing in the middle of this picture wearing a flying suit, organised a special airlift of groceries to be taken to his stand at the Arbroath Traders Exhibition. There visitors could sample his speciality tea and a new line of sausages. He also demonstrated Campbell's innovative new ready-to-serve soups. Convenience foods were still a rarity at this time. Provost Sir William Chapel, on the right, is seen receiving a package from the airlift from a little girl.

The Fit o' the Toon looking towards Union Street East, gaily decorated for the Coronation of King George VI and Queen Elizabeth on 12 May 1937. Arbroath's magistrates led a procession to the abbey for a service attended by 5,000 people, and this was followed by a salute of guns in Springfield Park. A flotilla of fishing boats lined up from the harbour to the Ness, and in the afternoon Arbroathians watched or participated in a procession of decorated lorries to the Victoria Park. At the park there were displays of dancing and gymnastics, a cycle maze and massed singing of Land of Hope and Glory. In the evening the townsfolk assembled to hear a broadcast by the new king, which was followed by more singing and dancing. The evening was finished off by a torchlight procession and bonfire.

Before the advent of electricity, locally-manufactured gas supplied energy to the home and for street lights. Reinstalling the lamps, which were repainted during the summer months, was a heavy job. Gas lamps were labour intensive, and needed to be individually lit and turned off each evening and morning by a leerie or lamplighter. The last gas lamp in Arbroath survived into the 1960s in Long Row, just off Guthrie Port, long after all the other lamps had been converted to electricity.

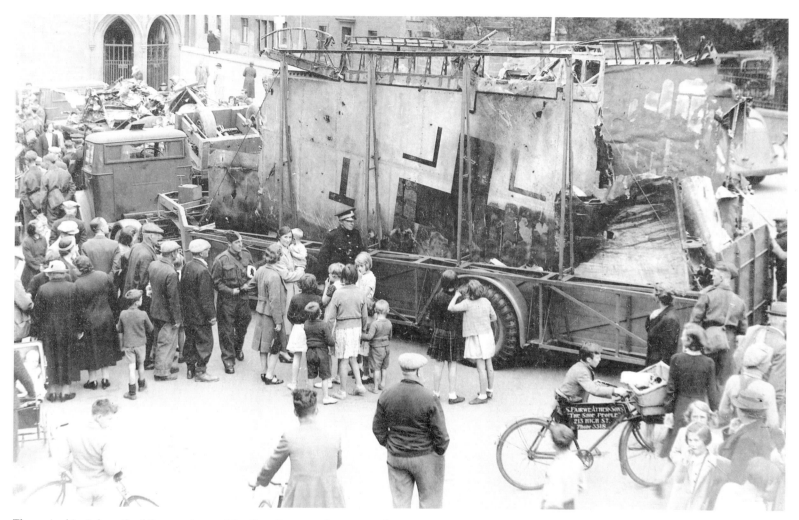

The arrival in Arbroath of the wreckage of the first German plane to crash in Scotland during World War II caused quite a sensation. Many local people turned out to watch it pass by, and it is seen here passing Arbroath Library on Hill Terrace. The Heinkel 115 seaplane crashed on 20 August 1940 on a farm at Arbirlot, killing the crew. Workers on the farm later told how the wreckage was spread so far and wide over the corn fields that the tractor-man had to constantly jump on and off his tractor to pick up the debris. The farm workers all took a souvenir from the seaplane.

Polish soldiers stationed in Arbroath in the early part of World War II parade past Provost Sir William Chapel and other dignitaries in front of the Town House. The parade was possibly associated with the visit of King George and Queen Elizabeth to the Polish soldiers' headquarters at the Elms in February 1941. During the Second World War, many Polish personnel were stationed across Angus under the command of General Zikorski.

The Arbroath Abbey Pageant was instituted in 1947 to commemorate the signing of the Declaration of Arbroath at the abbey on 6 April 1320. The historic events of that year were re-enacted by a large company of Arbroathians who prepared hundreds of authentic costumes for the pageant. This was held annually for ten years and then completed three further revivals. The pageant was successfully staged again in 1999 and 2000. A youthful Andy Stewart provided the voice of the prologue in the very first production. He went on to enjoy a long and distinguished career as a well-known Scottish entertainer and singer.

An Arbroath Co-operative Society float in Kirriemuir telling the story of the discovery of the Stone of Destiny before the High Altar of Arbroath Abbey on 11 April 1951. The stone had previously been stolen from Westminster Abbey and had been missing for several months. One of those responsible for its disappearance was Ian Hamilton, a friend of Hugh MacDiarmid, poet and fervent Scottish nationalist. MacDiarmid had gone to London in the early 1930s with the proclaimed aim of stealing the stone, but never got further than inspecting its security arrangements in Westminster Abbey. He decided it was too well guarded to steal and took comfort from his thwarted plans by talking about the project in every London pub he entered. His story may well have inspired his young friend to take action.

Egg Collection Day was a fund-raising campaign organised on behalf of Arbroath Infirmary. This picture shows someone in a policeman's costume stopping a motorcyclist in Keptie Street to demand a 'bribe'. Unfortunately, the date of the photograph is unknown, as is the event's connection with collecting eggs! Before the establishment of the National Health Service after World War II, hospitals were dependent on fund-raising and benefactors for their income. Arbroath's present hospital was erected in 1916 and at the time was considered to be 'thoroughly modern'. It was intended primarily for the poor of the community who received its services free of charge. The town council gifted the land it was built on, and the construction costs were raised by public subscription. An endowment fund to cover the running costs was also established. The total cost of building the new hospital was £14,693.

Arbroath's outdoor swimming pool was the leading tourist attraction in the town for many years. It was opened on Saturday 7 July 1934 and became a focus for holidaymakers of all ages, with swimming and diving competitions and roller skating displays amongst the activities organised. In the late 1960s and early 1970s the growing national trend towards sunshine holidays abroad led to the slow demise of Arbroath and other British seaside towns as mass holidays destinations. The pool closed in the 1980s and was filled in, although part of the facade has been retained and now houses a nightclub and a bowling alley.

Visitors admiring the work of Angus artist James Watterson Herald at an exhibition which opened in the art gallery at Arbroath Library on 6 July 1935. Herald was a highly talented exponent of watercolours and pastels with an extensive output of paintings. He was born in Forfar in 1859 and pursued an artistic education in Edinburgh and London before finally settling in Arbroath in 1901. He found his new home to be a great inspiration, and images of the abbey, harbour, fisherfolk and local crowd scenes dominate his work. During his lifetime his reputation was on a par with those of James Melville and Charles Whistler. Herald died in 1914.

In the early years of the twentieth century it was common for households to have milk delivered to their doors by local dairies. The cart would come round on a daily basis, and people would either take a jug or tin out to be filled up, or leave one hanging from a gatepost. Milk had to be supplied daily due to the lack of refrigeration. In this picture a local dairyman poses for a photograph with his family before starting his rounds. Beside his wife stands a giant water butt, perhaps indicating a love of gardening.

Before the advent of the motor car more affluent members of Arbroath society, such as mill owners, kept their own horse and carriage in stables adjoining their houses. Many of these stables can still be seen today having been converted into garages or even houses.

The Abbot's House, lying within the grounds of Arbroath Abbey, is one of the few surviving pre-Reformation ecclesiastical residences in Scotland. Its most famous occupant was Cardinal Beaton. Although it has been extended and altered greatly over the years, the core of the house dates from the thirteenth century. After the Reformation of the Roman Catholic Church in the sixteenth century, it became a struggle to find a use for the building. For many years it provided a manse for the parish minister and was later let to private tenants. Wallace, Gardyne & Co. rented the house in the eighteenth century for use as a thread factory, and it is during this period that many of its original features are believed to have been destroyed. In 1890 the town council bought the building and halted its decline into a ruinous condition.

The Glasite Church belonged to a sect founded by the Rev. John Glas of Tealing, and stood at the corner of Church Street and High Street. It was built in 1783 and demolished in January 1909. The church was more familiarly known as the Kail Kirkie because its parishioners travelled in from the country and had soup and something to eat while waiting for the afternoon service to begin. Following the church's demolition, the site was redeveloped into a three-storey drapery store for the Co-operative Society in 1911.

The minister of the Queen Street Congregational Church poses outside the manse with his wife and daughter at the turn of the twentieth century. The two-storey manse was built in 1883, and demolished *c.*1989. Afterwards the church's communion plate and chalice were donated to the Signal Tower Museum.

The Abbey School had accommodation for 350 pupils in seven classrooms, an average of 50 pupils per class. It closed in 1954 when it was amalgamated with Parkhouse School. The building was subsequently used by the Babygro Knitwear Company for a time, before being demolished to make way for the Abbey Health Centre.

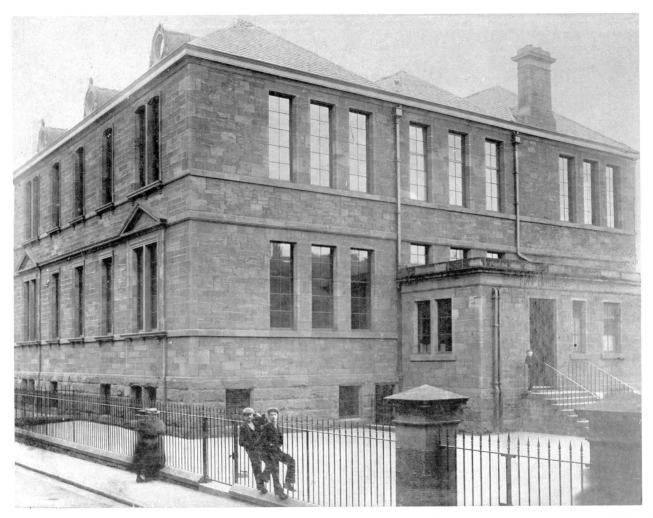

Many of Arbroath's Victorian schools have been torn down and replaced by modern buildings. Parkhouse School was erected in 1876 under the terms of the new Education Act of 1873 which sought to improve educational standards throughout Scotland. From the outset, Parkhouse was faced with overcrowding problems for which it was severely criticised by Her Majesty's Inspectors of Schools. The school closed in 1969 and was demolished in 1973 to make way for a supermarket car park.

A steam goods train passing over the railway bridge on the main road to Dundee neatly frames the old tollhouse. Toll roads and their associated tollhouses were in use from the late eighteenth century until 1879 when toll roads were abolished. Since that date some have been used as ordinary homes, while others have been demolished. In 1789 an Act of Parliament was passed on behalf of the Forfarshire Road Trustees empowering any seven landowners with an income over a certain level, and the magistrates of royal burghs to set tolls on particular roads to regain the money invested in them. Despite the charges levied, the quality of toll roads was frequently poor, with many being impassable except in good weather. The mud was often so deep that horses sank up to their bellies. Tollhouses were occupied by speculators who bid for the right to operate them, and then recouped the money by collecting the tolls. Many were ex-soldiers. Toll keepers also sold alcohol to thirsty travellers, and their houses were centres for the exchange of news and gossip.

ARBROATH MINIATURE RAILWAY

Arbroath's miniature railway has been a popular seaside attraction since its inauguration in 1935 by Matthew Kerr senior. The railway started life in a field on Kerr's farm near Dundee before moving to its permanent home in Arbroath. Major improvements were made after World War II: the gauge was widened, the track lengthened to a quarter of a mile, and a signal box, turntable and tunnel added. The wee trains made the change from steam to diesel in the early 1960s and suffered a dip in their popularity as a consequence, although the railway has since undergone a resurgence of popularity. The miniature railway has carried in excess of 1.5 million passengers since 1935.

Scaled-down diesel trains were introduced to the miniature railway in the early 1960s at the same time as steam trains were phased out. This was not a popular move with tourists. Between 1957 and 1959 Matthew Kerr senior also introduced a 'trackless' train known as the *Coronation Queen* which ran along the promenade. The engine was based on an American Santa Fe model and was built in Brighton by a well-known miniature railway craftsman, Ernie Johnston. The *Coronation Queen* spent only three summers in Arbroath before going to Bristol. This picture shows one of Kerr's trains giving its mainline counterpart, bound for Dundee, a run for its money.

KERR'S MINIATURE RAILWAYS, ARBROATH.

Apart from trains, Kerr provided other attractions for the wee traveller including buses which could carry about six passengers. A fire engine and a mini Strathtay Company bus still transport children along the Arbroath seafront today.

37

Arbroath was once served by two railway lines and two stations. The Ladyloan station was the terminus for the Dundee to Arbroath railway, which opened on 6 October 1838. Its construction was aided by both local merchants and landowners. Lord Panmure proved especially helpful and feued land for a nominal fee. On the day the line opened Arbroathians and folk from surrounding country districts came out en masse to watch the first train arrive. Dundee magistrates travelled to Arbroath to celebrate with local magistrates and landowners. Travelling on early railways was not always a comfortable affair, and open-air third class carriages were little different from cattle trucks. This picture shows the station in Keptie Road that is still in use today.

The present-day railway station on Keptie Road is adjacent to the site of the old Catherine Street station, which was the terminus of the Arbroath to Forfar line, opened on 3 January 1839. Arbroath's original stations (at Ladyloan and Catherine Street) were some distance apart, and a horse-drawn carriage ferried passengers between the two. The current station was rebuilt in 1911 on the site of an earlier ornate Victorian station, illustrated here. Catherine Street station was demolished in 1972.

Scott's Grocers, 195 High Street, celebrated its 80th anniversary in 1936. The shop was decorated for the occasion in the Victorian style of its origins. From the 1920s to 1966 Scott's was owned by Alexander Napier. Mrs Napier is the lady in the middle of the picture wearing the hat.

Keith Blackman's engineering business originated in the mid-nineteenth century as a tinsmith and gas fitters operation. It was a family concern and looked to the welfare of its workers. In 1893 James Keith introduced the 8 hour day, the first employer in Scotland to do so. Blackman's began to manufacture boilers and radiators in 1870, and in 1900 they merged with another company to become Keith Blackman Air Propellers Ventilating Company of America. The company's works once dominated the High Street, and the grandiose frontage shown in this photograph (decorated for the Coronation of Queen Elizabeth II in 1953) dated from 1910 when the works were rebuilt to house a number of machine shops and the company offices. The factory closed in 1965 and was subsequently demolished to allow the High Street to be widened.

Provost Colin Grant wearing court dress. Grant was a native of Aberlemno who came to Arbroath to open a shoemaking factory in 1862. His manufacturing and retail businesses flourished, and Grant used his wealth for charitable work, leading him to be described as 'Carnegie-ish'. He was a member of the Harbour Board, helped to acquire the Victoria Park for the town and laid out the Eliot golf course. Grant also served as a town councillor for many years and achieved the highest office of provost. During his time as chief magistrate he promoted the establishment of the public library and the public health hospital, and saw a new post office opened in Hill Street.

Hill Road was the location of Provost Grant's factory. Shoemaking had been a cottage industry in Arbroath until the arrival of Grant, who built a factory which employed 800 people to operate its steam powered machines. He not only manufactured shoes but also sold them through his own retail outlets in the town. The factory closed in 1923, and the building later enjoyed a new lease of life as the Marine Ballroom, which opened on Coronation Day 1937.

Workers treating yarn at Corsar's Mill on the Brothock Burn. By the late 1840s the first power looms for the weaving of sailcloth had been introduced to Arbroath by David Corsar, whose spinning manufactory dated back to 1790. The number of power looms increased rapidly and by the late nineteenth century the need for manual labour had dropped so much that a local movement emerged to assist redundant handloom weavers to emigrate. The sailcloth industry in Arbroath thrived until the rise of the steam ship, and in the twentieth century weaving companies moved into manufacturing synthetic fabrics. Francis Webster's factory, established in the late eighteenth century, was the last to survive and closed in the early 1990s.

Women workers spinning flax in Corsar's Mill. The factory has been decorated for the marriage of an unidentified Corsar son with evergreens, flags, and banners wishing the happy couple good luck and good health. Workers may have been lucky enough to have been given a day's paid holiday to celebrate the event.

Flax dressers, or 'drouthy hecklers', at Corsar's Mill holding hanks of flax. These workers pulled bundles of flax through progressively finer heckle pins until the fibres had become untangled and separated and were as soft and silky as human hair. The flax was then ready to spin. It was dusty work that made the workers very thirsty, hence the description 'drouthy'. Hecklers were well-known for their political awareness and the term 'heckling' derives from their willingness to make their views known.

Workers at Corsar's Mill on the occasion of the marriage of a member of the Corsar family. All of the girls are wearing floral decorations. Corsar's was one of 34 mills and factories operating in Arbroath by 1875. By this time there were 1,100 power looms and 40,000 spindles in use, making Arbroath the second most important linen weaving town in Scotland. Wages varied according to the state of the industry and dropped during times of depression. Women and girls received lower wages than their male counterparts.

The view from the Stanley Foundry cupola looking towards the spire of St Mary's Episcopal Church. The strange shaped building to the left was the local gasworks. The chimney in the centre has now been demolished.

Nelson of Arbroath operated this Albion charabanc between Montrose, Lunan, Inverkeilor and Arbroath in the mid to late 1920s.

Later Nelson joined forces with another operator to become Hunter and Nelson of Victoria Garage, Arbroath. ASR 766 was an Albion Victor built in 1937 with a body by Cowieson of Glasgow. Hunter and Nelson ran a variety of local bus services around Arbroath and also a service from Arbroath to Brechin.